Social Skills

for primary pupils 2

**Seven one-hour sessions to help
pupils develop social
awareness and personal responsibility**

Deborah Cohen and Lorrae Jaderberg

Permission to photocopy

This book contains materials which may be reproduced by
photocopier or other means for use by the purchaser. This
permission is granted on the understanding that these copies will
be used within the educational establishment of the purchaser.
This book and all its contents remain copyright. Copies may be
made without reference to the publisher or to the licensing
scheme for the making of photocopies operated by the
Publishers' Licensing Agency.

The rights of Deborah Cohen and Lorrae Jaderberg to be
identified as authors of this work have been asserted by them in
accordance with sections 77 and 78 of the Copyright, Designs
and Patents Act 1988.

Social Skills for Primary Pupils 2
MT10775
ISBN-13: 978 1 85503 449 5

Printed in China for LDA,
Pintail Close, Victoria Business Park, Nottingham, NG4 2SG

Contents

About the authors

Deborah Cohen

Deborah Cohen is an advisory teacher for pupils with autism. She has a post-graduate diploma in specific learning difficulties and was a SENCo in two primary schools. Deborah has also worked for Parent Partnership, advising parents of children with special educational needs, and was a primary teacher in Barnet, north London, for 20 years.

Lorrae Jaderberg

Lorrae Jaderberg is an educational consultant. She has previously held posts as a deputy head teacher and inclusion manager at a north London primary school, a SENCo and a class teacher.

Acknowledgements

Dr Alan Cooklin

MB, ChB, FRC Psych

Alan is a consultant child and adolescent psychiatrist and consultant in family psychiatry at the University College London Hospitals. He developed, wrote and produced the training tool, Being Seen and Heard: The Needs of Children With Parents With Mental Health Illness.

Colin McGee

DipPsych, UKCP Reg, DHpPsych (UK), GQHP, RegHyp (GHR) CertEd

Brookland Junior School, London

Heather Blackmore (head teacher) and the pupils and staff who were involved in the piloting of the Social Skills for Primary Pupils programme.

Hyde School

Di Jolley and Claudette Brown for their helpful evaluations.

Introduction

What is Social Skills for Primary Pupils 2?

Social Skills for Primary Pupils is a programme to help children develop social awareness and understanding of their interactions and responsibilities regarding their own and others' behaviour.

Over seven sessions, pupils build up personal experience through discussion, games and exercises informed by adult and peer feedback. Sessions cover National Curriculum PSHE and Citizenship guidelines. The Primary National Strategy (*Excellence and Enjoyment: Learning and Teaching in the Primary Years*) affirms a vision for primary education that recognises the importance of social skills in creating effective conditions for learning. The following skills are included:

- knowing when to talk, what to talk about and when to hold back;
- knowing how to take turns fairly;
- taking feedback without getting upset, and giving feedback without causing offence;
- being able to say sorry and mean it;
- knowing how to resolve conflict, and understanding that conflict is a normal part of life;
- being able to reflect accurately on what is happening and modify approaches as necessary;
- being able to join/lead a group;
- knowing the local rules of argument, debate and conversation;

- knowing how your strengths complement those of pupils you are working and learning with;
- being able to share information and ideas;
- developing confidence and responsibility and making the most of your abilities;
- developing relationships and respecting the differences between people;
- promoting active listening.

> **Clear structure, clear aims and the activities are well thought out.**

> **The programme is laid out in a logical order and is very easy to follow.**

Why was the programme developed?

Social Skills for Primary Pupils was developed as part of inclusive primary practice. There is a growing need for social skills intervention in the primary years. This programme is designed for use with a small group, but may be adapted for whole-class use. Groups should consist of six to eight pupils and include model pupils, quiet pupils and one pupil, or two with complementary needs.

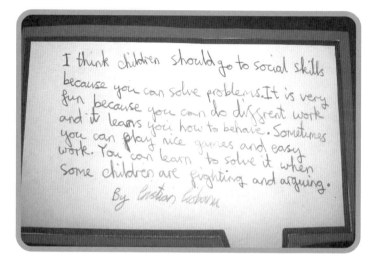

During the sessions the pupils learn about their strengths and weaknesses and how these help them grow and develop. Pupils learn from their peers and adult supporter by a process of gradual, heightened self-awareness. They learn how to deal with their specific weaknesses and with issues relating to conflict resolution, friendships and behaviour in the playground and in class.

This programme may lead on to further specialised group or one-to-one work, either in school or provided by outside agencies.

What is behind it?

It is understood that pupils' self-esteem and social and emotional well-being is central to their ability to fulfil their academic, social and emotional potential. The Primary National Strategy suggests that many primary pupils struggle with social and emotional issues which significantly affect their confidence and ability to perform to their own satisfaction at school. Using our own experience and informed by current research, we have designed this programme to support the learning of complex social interactions in school.

> **66 Children realised the impact of their actions on other people. 99**

Every Child Matters (DCFS) emphasises the prevention of difficulties in children's lives and highlights the crucial role of schools. This programme addresses many of its aims.

How does it work?

We know that children, like adults, are motivated and learn best when they feel safe and in control of their learning. *Social Skills for Primary Pupils* is designed to enable pupils to develop an understanding of the themes of the sessions and learn strategies to deal with issues. Elements of the programme may be adapted to suit individual situations and needs.

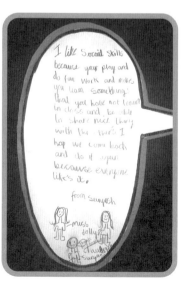

> **They really looked forward to our sessions together and were sorry when the programme ended.** 》

> **For some pupils, it was the first opportunity they had ever had to speak about their thoughts and feelings.** 》

> **It was very easy to administer.** 》

Why does it work?

This programme builds on individual and group trust, confidentiality and peer/adult support. It allows pupils to explore relevant challenging social and emotional issues in safety. Guidelines, boundaries and contracts are agreed at the start and the operating rules of the group are made clear, creating a safe emotional and physical environment.

The sessions are structured and paced in such a way that pupils will operate from their own level of personal development. By the second session pupils relax as they recognise the familiar framework of the previous session. They begin to build up trust, which enables them to utilise the framework to support experimentation with their new social skills in a safe environment. This also provides ongoing opportunity for self-evaluation, challenge and target-setting to take place.

A generous reward system provides regular, measured and positive feedback throughout the sessions. As a result, pupils' self-esteem and motivation increase as they build on their successes and look forward to the next session and the challenges it will bring. By the end of the seven sessions, pupils report that they feel more confident in dealing with specific issues and have a clearer understanding of how their own strengths and weaknesses affect them. They develop additional strategies to support themselves.

What does the programme consist of?

The programme consists of seven 50-minute sessions (allowing a little leeway in a one-hour session). These may be held over days, weeks or months. Each session has an adult's script, an adult evaluation grid, targets and a homework task. A pupil questionnaire is completed before the programme starts and ends and a pupil evaluation sheet is completed during the last session.

Each session focuses on specific issues presented in short activities – games, discussions, problem-solving, collaborative reflection, working in pairs and creating conclusions. The activities are designed to help pupils relax and bond as a group, and to stimulate discussion. There is a homework reinforcement activity, using petals of a flower, which pupils complete to form a final presentation. If a pupil has difficulty completing the homework task, an opportunity may be provided during the school day for it to be completed.

To reinforce positive contributions, stickers are given as a reward for collecting ticks during the session. During the first two sessions a group contract is developed and signed by all group members (including the adult facilitator). It is read at the beginning of each session.

At the end of each session, the adult supporter evaluates the session, makes comments and scores the individual pupil's contributions on the Adult evaluation grid. These evaluations form a valuable record which may be helpful for the class teacher, outside agencies, educational psychologist and parents. They may also be used as evidence for planning and developing future social skills work.

> **It emphasised the positive rather than the negative.**

During Sessions 6 and 7, all of the homework petals are put together and the pupils create a poster. This takes the form of a flower in a pot with a watering can watering the flower. Each part of the poster symbolises an aspect of the sessions and when completed it provides a positive reminder of all that has been achieved. It also serves as an evaluation tool as the pupils show the depth of their understanding of the sessions. The pupils are usually very proud of their poster. Their work may be displayed – ask pupils if they mind having their work displayed publicly. Some may decline as this may be sensitive and private work. Adults should emphasise that to decline is acceptable.

A certificate of achievement is presented to successful participants as an acknowledgement of their efforts. A small gift may also be presented.

The Pupil questionnaire should be filled in before the programme starts. The class teacher may give pupils this task for homework or it may be completed in school. The adult

supporter may sit with each pupil to help them complete the questionnaire as this creates a working alliance. The Pupil evaluation sheet will be completed as part of the last session. This information may be used as an indication of the pupils' areas of strengths and weaknesses and to inform future planning.

Who should run the group?

As this is a complex area of primary children's development, it is recommended that someone with experience in dealing with conflict resolution, mediation and self-esteem issues runs the group. This may be a member of staff whose personal or professional strengths lie in this area, such as a trained counsellor, teaching assistant, support teacher, SENCo, deputy head or head teacher.

Sessions are designed to be led and evaluated by one person. Schools may choose to run sessions with two adults, one leading the session and the other observing and taking notes for evaluation purposes. This offers an opportunity to train new adults to run groups. Some schools have found it beneficial to run all of the groups with two adults so that, in the event of a pupil raising painful or distressing issues during a session, one adult can support the individual pupil whilst the other adult continues with the group.

The benefits of the programme are greatest when it forms part of a whole-school approach. Ideally all staff should be included in an initial training session which explains the aims and methodology so that they can help pupils to transfer skills learned within the group into different settings in school. At the very least, all teachers and teaching assistants working directly with pupils in the group should be briefed about the programme and be made aware of pupils' targets so that they can support and encourage those pupils in acting appropriately in school.

❝ It was easy to adapt if necessary. ❞

In one school, the class teacher picked up a theme from the group (disrupting the class) and adapted it for the whole class during PSHE (see p. 58). She used the pupils' targets to create a large tree. Pupils decorated and wrote on a leaf which they stuck on a branch each time they were helpful in class.

They created a 'tree of harmony' in the corner of their classroom.

When and where should the sessions take place?

Group sessions can take place at a time the class teacher judges to be appropriate. Whole-class sessions should be planned as part of the PSHE curriculum (see p. 58). Group sessions should take place in a private and quiet environment.

How do you choose a primary target pupil?

When a pupil is having social or emotional difficulties in school that are a serious cause of concern for the parent, teaching assistant, class teacher, SENCo or the pupil themselves, these pupils may benefit from being part of a group. Sometimes pupils' self-esteem may be affected by problems outside school rather than by a specific school-based issue. Pupils in this category will also benefit from this form of social skills intervention.

There are no hard and fast rules about which pupils to choose. Use professional judgement according to the individual situations and needs. The group should be chosen to support and complement the needs of the target children.

Elements of self-esteem

During the seven sessions the programme addresses various elements of self-esteem, such as:

- unconditional self-acceptance
- sense of capability and purpose
- appropriate assertiveness
- experience of flow and fulfilment
- sense of responsibility and accountability
- sense of safety and security
- sense of belonging
- sense of integrity.

❝ There were lots of opportunities to talk. ❞

Challenge, inclusion, learning styles and self-evaluation

Central to *Social Skills for Primary Pupils 2* is inclusive practice. Pupils are able to access the materials and are challenged at the level appropriate for them. This is a multi-sensory programme and we have found that it suits all learning styles. Pupils with English as an additional language are encouraged to ask for help if necessary in understanding the tasks and can be prepared ahead of time with vocabulary rehearsal. Words on petals may be written in a pupil's home language and a translated version can be presented alongside. The adult running the group may adapt the language used in the script according to the needs of the group with which they are working. Some schools have found it helpful to adapt or simplify the language in the photocopiable masters for specific pupils.

Developing self-evaluation skills is a key part of the programme. Pupils are encouraged to consider perceptions of themselves and their behaviour alongside peers' views in order to develop and build an accurate picture of themselves, their social skills and their strengths and weaknesses. This is about building and strengthening the 'observing self' within each child, promoting empathy and a sense of community.

At the end of the programme, some pupils may mark themselves down in some areas when completing the Pupil questionnaire. In discussion they may explain that they marked themselves too high at the start of the programme as they didn't have an accurate understanding of their own abilities.

Starting a group

Step 1

Explain the purpose of the sessions to the class teacher and ask for their help to select the group (**PCM 1**). Decide together when and where the group will meet. The general purpose will be to support and develop the social skills of two (perhaps one) pupils who have been identified as needing this intervention. The two pupils should have complementary needs. Quiet, reserved pupils are included to develop their assertiveness. Model pupils are chosen in order to demonstrate the appropriate responses to the exercises in each session and to reduce the possibility of the group being identified as a 'naughty group'.

The group might therefore comprise:

- primary target pupil and secondary target pupil
- two 'quiet' pupils
- two model pupils.

The group should consist of a similar number of boys and girls.

It is important to maintain the balance of the group as outlined. Groups should contain a maximum of two 'target' pupils to be effective.

66 The programme is laid out in a logical order and is very easy to follow. 99

66 There was a positive response from all the parents, who helped to reinforce the programme at home. 99

Letter to parents/carers and Pupil questionnaires

Once pupils have been chosen, a letter should be sent to parents/carers explaining the programme and homework, and seeking permission for the pupil to attend (**PCM 2**). Explain to parents of model pupils if necessary that their child will benefit from the acknowledgement and development of their skills. Once permission has been granted, send a personal invitation to each pupil (**PCM 3**). The class teacher should explain the Pupil questionnaires (**PCM 4**) to the pupils who join and give them out for completion. Check that all permissions have been given before starting.

Step 2

Start the sessions.

The content and order of the sessions is flexible and open to adaptation according to the needs of individual pupils and the group. Additional sessions may also be incorporated.

These sessions may be used as they are or as a template for sessions focusing on other issues. After becoming familiar with the programme, some schools have adapted the content to reflect issues specific to their individual circumstances.

Marking and evaluation

The register should be taken at the beginning of each session and a note made regarding homework completion. After each session, the Adult evaluation grid (**PCM 5**) should be completed and each pupil's scores noted. There should be a grid for each pupil. The grid records, on a scale of 1 to 5 (with 1 being lowest), the role and participation of each pupil during each session.

Pupils' roles within the group may be defined as group leader, group member, follower, disrupter, participant, aggressor, scapegoat, and so on. Roles may change within a session and from session to session. The Adult evaluation grids provide an overview of pupils' roles, participation and behaviour as perceived by the adult taking the group. This information may be used as evidence of pupils' progression and development.

The adult should evaluate their own input after each session and make notes for the next session.

The pupils receive up to 3 ticks after each activity from the adult: 1 for good listening, 1 for good sitting and 1 for their contribution. Every set of 9 ticks is worth a sticker, which should be provided by the adult. These should be given out generously to encourage as much confidence and self-esteem building as possible. Ticks outstanding at the end of a session should be carried over to the next session and count towards the next sticker. Pupils may also wish to peer nominate.

The ticks and stickers should be placed at the bottom of the signed contract during or at the end of each session from Session 2 onwards. The contracts may be presented to the pupils in Session 7.

Evaluation and follow-up

For some pupils, the social skills group is the first opportunity they will have to examine their own feelings and have others value their experiences and ideas. Many schools will be keen to build on this positive experience and to give pupils further opportunities to develop their personal growth.

During the course of the social skills programme, you will have accumulated a great deal of information about the pupils from:

- pupils themselves – through their participation in the group
- your own informal observations
- the Adult evaluation grid for each pupil
- the Pupil questionnaire at the beginning and end of the programme and the Pupil evaluation sheet at the end
- the content of the finished posters.

On the basis of this evidence, and in line with the whole-school approach, schools may decide that further school-based intervention would be helpful for specific pupils, examples of which are described on page 58.

The records may also be used as evidence in making a referral to outside agencies such as an educational psychologist, a counsellor or child and adolescent mental health services.

Most pupils who complete the programme successfully will continue to develop the skills they have learned in the group and, in doing so, maximise their ability to operate effectively within the school environment. However, schools may decide that further intervention is required for specific pupils. Some of the follow-up work undertaken by schools is described below:

- Follow-up sessions were held a few weeks later to see how pupils were managing changes made.

- A pupil was referred to other agencies for in-depth therapeutic input.

- A pupil was given additional one-to-one time to practise strategies to use in the classroom and playground.

- A parenting class was set up to run parallel to the social skills group. Parents addressed similar themes to those in the social skills group and were therefore able to support the work of the school by ensuring a consistent approach at home.

- A school followed up the programme by offering a 'talk time' in which pupils could book a 15-minute slot with the group leader to talk about issues that were of concern to them or to spend time reinforcing the work that had been done in the group.

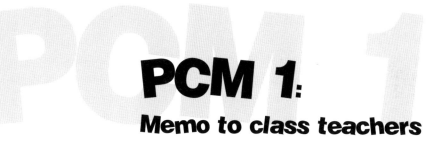

SOCIAL SKILLS GROUP

To: Class: Date:

From:

<u>Re: Social Skills Group</u>

The target pupil for this group is ....

Please would you choose other children to join the group.

This group will start on ....

The group will meet for seven one-hour sessions.

Two model pupils ....

Two quiet pupils ....

One other pupil who would benefit from a social skills group

....

Please advise your preferred time for the group to meet:

Day of week ....   Lesson ....

Please return this form by ....

Thank you.

PCM 2:
Letter to inform parents/carers

Date:

DEAR PARENT/CARER

<u>Re: Social Skills Group</u> – <u>Class</u> ...

Your child has been chosen to participate in a PSHE programme as part of the PSHE/Citizenship curriculum.

The groups consist of about six children who will work together with me for seven one-hour sessions. We shall focus on areas such as developing friendships, self-awareness, confidence, understanding others, feeling valued and accepted as part of a group, problem-solving and reflection.

The children have been chosen to complement each other. They practise desired behaviour, contribute to thought-provoking discussion and are encouraged to give appropriate feedback. They will be encouraged to work together as a group, sharing ideas and building up good relationships with each other.

There are homework assignments each week and I should be grateful if you would ensure this work is completed and returned the following week.

If you do not wish your child to participate in this group, please let me know as soon as possible so that another pupil may be offered the place. The children will attend sessions on

....

....

If you would like further information, please contact me.

I am looking forward to working with your child.

Yours sincerely

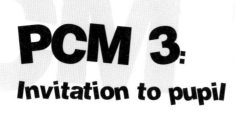

Dear

Class ...

You have been chosen to take part in a PSHE group starting on

....

Your group will consist of ... children who will be working together for seven one-hour sessions, concentrating on friendships, understanding others, working as part of a group and problem-solving.

There will be interesting discussions, activities and games.

There will be homework assignments each time, in which you will create a poster to keep.

This is a special opportunity you are being offered. It is only for selected children.

Sessions will take place at ....

I am looking forward to working with you.

Yours

PCM 4:
Pupil questionnaire

Name: ....

Date: ....

For each statement, circle the picture that shows how you feel.

I am able to express my feelings.	☹	☹	😐	🙂	😊
I feel confident.	☹	☹	😐	🙂	😊
I am able to listen.	☹	☹	😐	🙂	😊
I am able to understand other people's feelings.	☹	☹	😐	🙂	😊
I am able to deal with difficult situations.	☹	☹	😐	🙂	😊
I feel part of the group/class.	☹	☹	😐	🙂	😊
Other people understand me.	☹	☹	😐	🙂	😊
I have fun and play with others.	☹	☹	😐	🙂	😊

Permission to Photocopy

PCM 5:
Adult evaluation grid

Pupil's name: ....

Score columns on a 1–5 scale (1 being low and 5 being high). Describe role within group: leader (L), group member (GM), follower (F), disrupter (D), participant (P), aggressor (A), scapegoat (S).

Session number	Attendance and homework	Describe role within group	Relationship with peers 1–5 scale	Response to adults 1–5 scale	Joining in activities 1–5 scale	Comments
1						
2						
3						
4						
5						
6						
7						

Session 1 Establishing ground rules

Resources

- Adult evaluation grid (**PCM 5**) – one per pupil
- Sample contract (**PCM 6**)   stickers   pencils   crayons
- Pupil self-portrait (**PCM 7**) – one per pupil
- Homework sheet (**PCM 8**) – one per pupil

Aims

- To break the ice, make everyone feel comfortable and welcome
- To enable the group to begin to form and develop a common understanding and purpose
- To establish ground rules for the group to function
- To begin to think about themselves and their responsibilities for their actions
- To ensure that they want to come back next time, by making the session as much fun and as relaxed as possible

Introduction 5 mins.

Take the register, and say hello to everyone in the group.

During the lesson up to 3 ticks will be given for each activity; for good sitting, for good listening and for good work. If you get 9 ticks, you will receive a sticker. The stickers will be added to contracts next week.

Who will remind everyone of what I just said?

Give out ticks for responses.

Game: Introducing myself 5 mins.

This game establishes communication and boosts self-confidence.

Each of you will introduce yourselves to your neighbours, like this:

'I am ... To my left is ... To my right is ...'.

Model the activity by going first:

My name is Mrs Jones. To my left is Jamal. To my right is Anna.

Once everyone in the group understands the activity, go around the group in turn, following the same routine.

Give out ticks as appropriate.

Game: Oranges and Lemons 5 mins.

The aim is for pupils to learn to listen and keep each other safe. Number off as 'oranges' and 'lemons'.

Move to a new place if your fruit is called. Do not move back to the same place in the next go. If I say 'fruit salad', everyone has to move.

Pupils move places according to what you say. Give out ticks for this part of the session.

Setting the ground rules 10 mins.

Pupils learn why it is necessary to have rules in school. Choose one of the following options, depending on how the previous game was played.

If the game was calm and orderly:

We didn't make any rules about the game: everyone observed some rules without discussion. What rules did we apply during Oranges and Lemons?

Together make an oral list of rules that were applied. Give out ticks.

If the game was rowdy:

We can see from the game that we need rules to work well together, feel comfortable and safe and enjoy the game.

What rules should we use for this game?

Together make an oral list of rules to keep. Give out ticks.

During the next six sessions we shall be working together and talking about things that are important to us, and how we feel. We shall be asking others to help us think of ideas to solve any problems we have in the classroom or in the playground. We need some rules. Can anyone suggest some?

Each pupil suggests rules. All of the group say if they agree with it by a show of hands. Establish at least 4–5 rules.

Encourage pupils to include the following:

- Listening when other people are talking.

- Respecting the things children share about themselves in this group.

- Using the term 'someone' instead of their name when talking about other children – just say 'In the playground someone …'.

Show the Sample contract to the group. Discuss the rules set out in the Sample contract. Do they understand what it means when they sign something? Give out ticks.

❝Listening is harder than I thought.❞

Mia (7 yrs)

Starting a flower `5 mins.`

Explain to the group how the flower will be created.

Over the next six sessions, you are all going to make your own flower. Each petal will have writing or drawing on it about the things we are working on. In the middle of the flower will be a drawing of yourself, which we are going to do today.

In the last session we shall put together all the petals and assemble the flower to show how hard we have worked and how far we have grown since the sessions started.

> **"At the beginning I thought I could do this really well, but in the end I realised it was quite difficult."**
>
> *Emi (8 yrs)*

Self-portrait `10 mins.`

This activity is designed to build self-esteem, self-confidence and communication skills.

Give out the Pupil self-portrait sheet, pencils and crayons. Each pupil should complete their self-portrait, and add their name underneath the picture.

When the pictures are finished, ask each pupil to show their picture and describe themselves, saying something positive about their own personality and how they see themselves. Then ask the group to make suggestions. The pupil can use the suggestions on their homework petal. Complete this part of the session by giving out ticks.

Homework `5 mins.`

Give each pupil a copy of the Homework sheet for Session 1 with their own positive statement written on it.

Explain that before the next session they should write on their petal three times when they have fitted this description. They should decorate their petal, cut it out and bring it to the next session.

End game `5 mins.`

Play Oranges and Lemons again – fast. Before you begin, ask the group:

Who can remember the rules?

Evaluate the session using the Adult evaluation grid – one for each pupil. Add comments each week to build a pupil profile over the programme.

Social Skills Group Contract

- We put up our hands to speak and we take turns.

- When someone is speaking, we listen.

- We sit correctly in our chairs.

- We look at each other when we speak and we respect what people say.

Signed .... Signed ....

Signed .... Signed ....

Signed .... Signed ....

Signed .... Signed ....

Date.................................

PCM 7: Pupil self-portrait

Draw your self-portrait inside this oval.

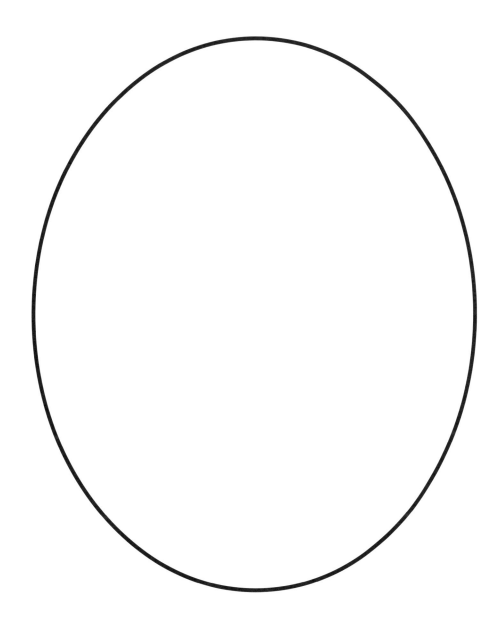

My name is:...

PCM 8:
Homework sheet Session 1

Name:..

During our first session you were described as:

....

In the petal, write down three times during the week when you fitted this description. You may decorate your petal if you want. Cut out your petal and bring it to our next session.

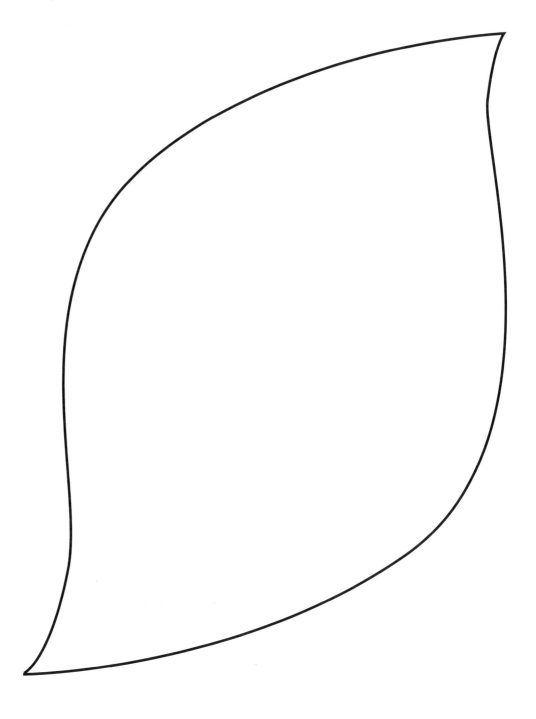

Session 2 Learning about one another

Resources

- stickers
- pencils
- Adult evaluation grids
- Group contract (**PCM 9**) – one per pupil
- Homework sheet (**PCM 10**) – one per pupil

Aims

- To consolidate ground rules by which the group functions
- To think about how they see themselves and how others see them
- To begin to be aware of how other people respond to their actions

Introduction 1 min.

Take the register and greet everyone. Remind pupils of the tick system: they earn up to three ticks for good sitting, good listening and good work. Nine ticks will be rewarded with a sticker.

Game: The Storm 5 mins.

This is a group-building activity.

Start making a noise, e.g. wind. The noise builds as pupils are encouraged to join in one by one and maintain the sound. Add in new sounds – e.g. rain, trees – which the pupils take up in turn around the group until the sound of the storm builds to a maximum. Led by you, the sounds eventually die away to a quiet pit-a-pat of rain. Sounds can be made orally or by using fingers, hands, knees, etc.

Complete the activity by giving out ticks.

Signing contracts and discussing rules 10 mins.

Pupils establish an agreed way of working co-operatively and develop communication skills.

Pupils discuss the rules set out on the Group contract, as agreed in the last session. How will they help the group to work together?

Give a contract to each pupil. All agree and sign each copy of the Contract. The adult also signs. Pupils add stickers collected to date to their own contract.

Complete the activity by giving out ticks.

Game: Pass the Animal Noise `5 mins.`

This activity promotes active listening and provides an opportunity to practise sticking to agreed rules.

A pupil makes an animal noise which the other pupils take turns to copy. Go around the circle until each pupil has had a turn to make their own animal noise.

Review homework `10 mins.`

This activity is designed to build self-esteem, and to practise effective communication skills and turn taking.

Ask each pupil in turn to read out what they wrote on their homework sheet. Discuss how they felt when they behaved that way and how others responded to them.

What did you learn from your homework?

Emphasise that if you behave in a positive way, the response to you is usually positive.

Give out ticks as usual.

Activity: The good things people can see in me are ... `15 mins.`

This activity focuses on raising the self-esteem of themselves and others, and on improving self-confidence and communication skills.

Ask the group to think of the good qualities of each of the other members. Encourage pupils to give examples, e.g. '[Maisie] is very kind because she always looks out for me at lunchtime.' When the group have had their say, ask a pupil 'What do you think about this?' encouraging self-reflection and acknowledgement of their good qualities. Give each pupil a copy of the Homework sheet so they can record the positive qualities identified by the group – for example, 'kind'. If necessary, write this for the child.

Record the qualities ascribed to each child on the Adult evaluation grid.

Give out ticks for this part of the session.

66 I've learned to play better with my friends. **99**

Sam (8 yrs)

66 It's much harder than I thought, I'm more careful – I care about how I talk to people now. Looking for solutions is difficult, this group has helped me under-stand people better. **99**

Vaishnav (9 yrs)

Homework 5 mins.

Explain to the pupils that before next time they need to write on the petal on the Homework sheet one sentence for each word, describing one thing that they did that showed these good things.

For example, for 'kind': 'Someone was on their own in the playground so I invited them to join our game.'

They should also write down how the other person responded, then decorate the petal and bring it to the next session.

Give out ticks.

End game: *If I were an animal, I would be ... because ...* 5 mins.

This game concludes the session by encouraging self-reflection.

Ask the pupils to think of a positive quality they have, or would like to have. Which animal has this quality? The adult models the activity first:

If I were an animal, I would be a lion because they are brave and I want to be brave.

Go around the group, asking for a contribution from each pupil.

Keep a note of answers on the Adult evaluation grid. Evaluate the session using these grids.

Social Skills Group Contract

- We put up our hands to speak and we take turns.
- We listen when someone else is speaking.
- We make eye contact to show we are listening.
- We care for each other.
- We try to understand each other.
- We sit correctly in our chairs.
- We keep the group's business private.

Signed .... Signed ....

Signed .... Signed ....

Signed .... Signed ....

Signed .... Signed ....

Date.......................................

PCM 10:
Homework sheet Session 2

Fill in this sheet the day before Session 3.

Name:..

During our session other people described you as:

....

For each of these words, write in the petal one thing you did since Session 2 that showed these good things. Don't write down names, just say 'someone'.

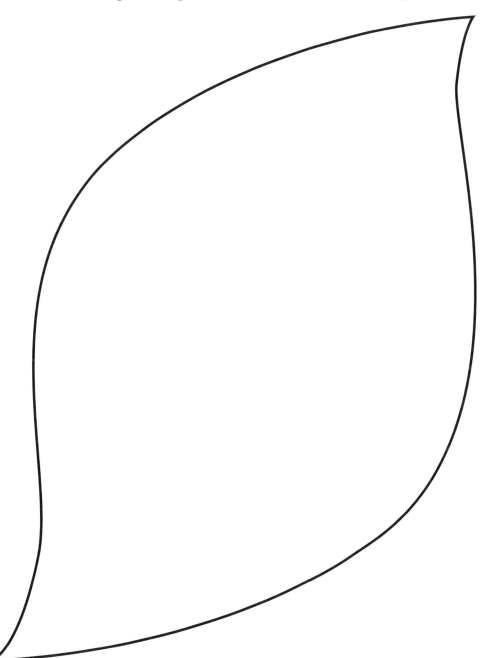

Example:

Someone was on their own in the playground so I invited them to join in our game.

Write down how the other person responded. You may decorate your petal if you want. Cut out your petal and bring it to our next session.

Permission to Photocopy

Session 3 Problem-solving

Resources

- Situation cards (**PCM 11**)
- Homework sheet (**PCM 12**) – one per pupil
- Group contracts • Adult evaluation grids • pencils • stickers

Aims

- To consider why friends are important
- To recognise how conflict can arise with friends, and possible solutions
- To understand that there is more than one solution to a problem

Introduction 1 min.

Take the register, greet everyone and remind pupils of the tick system.

Game: The Storm 5 mins.

Repeat this game from Session 2. This is a useful group-building activity. This time you could ask a pupil to explain how to play the game, or choose a pupil to lead. Give out ticks as appropriate at the end.

Remind the group of their contracts 5 mins.

Discuss the rules agreed in the contracts with the children.

Who can remember what the rules are?

This will establish an agreed, co-operative way of working, and develop communication skills.

Give out contracts. Award any stickers from the previous session to stick on their contracts. Finish by giving out ticks.

Review homework 10 mins.

This activity builds self-esteem and communication skills and practises taking turns.

Each pupil chooses one sentence from their petal to read out. Pupils say why they have chosen that sentence, e.g. 'I was pleased with the way I dealt with it', 'The other person thanked me', 'I changed my mind about something and it was OK', and so on. ▶▶▶

▶▶▶ Tell the children:

The way we behave affects the way other people behave towards us. We can change the way people respond to us by the approach we take towards them.

For example, if my friend is shouting at me, I can shout back and then we end up having an argument. If my friend is shouting at me, I can talk quietly and say 'I can see you are upset, let's talk about the problem and try and find a solution ...' – or I can walk away.

End the session by giving out ticks.

Activity: I like to have friends because ... 2 mins.

This activity promotes self-reflection and practises communication skills.

Introduce the activity by saying:

Friends are important to us and we should try to work things out with them. Why are friends important? Why do we like to have friends?

Introduce an extra rule for this discussion: do not mention any names.

Go round the circle. Each person says 'I like to have friends because ...'. Model the activity first. Encourage the children to think of statements with reasons rather than simple words such as 'They are nice.' For example, 'I like to have friends because they play skipping with me at lunchtime / they cheer me up when I'm feeling miserable.'

Conclude the activity by giving out ticks.

Discussion: Why do friends fall out? 5 mins.

This activity encourages children to reflect on and express their feelings. Ask the group:

Why don't friends always agree?

Why do we sometimes fall out with friends?

Ask the children to suggest their ideas. Remind them of the extra rule: do not mention any names. Their suggestions may include:

- different points of view
- different likes/dislikes
- misunderstandings
- stubbornness
- unkindness
- selfishness
- some children are more adventurous/outgoing than others.

How does it feel if you are in conflict / not friends with / having an argument / have fallen out with someone else?

Take ideas from the whole group. Suggestions may include feeling upset, hurt, miserable or alone.

We don't always have to agree with our friends – we respect each other's differences.

End the activity by giving out ticks.

❝ I've learned about difficult situations – fights between other people. ❞

Sally (8 yrs)

Activity: Resolving conflicts `10 mins.`

Through this activity, children learn to recognise that there is more than one solution to a problem and to consider different points of view. They will also practise conflict resolution skills.

Divide the group into pairs and give each pair a situation card. These cards describe situations where conflict may arise.

1. A wants to watch a cartoon on television. B wants to watch a game show. The two programmes are both on at the same time.

2. A and B both want to read the same reading book.

3. A wants to play with B in the playground, but B is already playing with C.

Ask the children to think of ways of resolving the conflict and discuss these with their partner.

There may be more than one way of solving the problem. How many different ways can you think of?

Ask each pair to report back to the group, explaining the ideas they have had. The other pairs may have other suggestions.

There is always more than one solution to a problem. Rather than getting into an argument, you may be able to try a different approach to solving a problem.

Give out the ticks for this activity.

Open forum `10 mins.`

This is an opportunity for pupils to explore different solutions to real problems, encouraging self-expression, problem-solving, listening skills and taking turns.

Tell the children that this part of the session is for discussing any problems with friends that they may need help with.

Reinforce the rules for this activity:

- No names – say 'someone'

- In offering ideas, children should say 'Would it help if ...', or 'Would it help if I ...'

- In response, a child can answer 'Thank you, I will try that / I've tried that ...' and report back next time.

If no one has a problem to share, present the following problem:

I have a friend who likes to monopolise me. She doesn't like me to see my other friends. She always wants to know what I'm doing and who I was with. I like her very much but I like my other friends too.

Give out ticks as appropriate at the end of the activity.

Social Skills for Primary Pupils 2

Homework 5 mins.

This activity involves children in looking at action and consequence.

Give out Homework sheets.

Explain to pupils that during the next week they need to describe an occasion when they might have fallen out with a friend, brother or sister, but they did something which solved the problem. They should not mention names, just write 'someone'. Their description should include:

- what the problem was
- what they did to solve the problem
- how the other person felt afterwards
- how they felt afterwards and why.

They should then decorate their petal, cut it out and bring it to the next session.

Give out ticks for this part of the session.

End game: Tangles 5 mins.

Ask everyone to stand in a circle and close their eyes. Pupils reach across the circle and hold hands with two different people who are not standing next to them. The group's hands will be tangled together. Pupils open their eyes.

Challenge the group to untangle themselves without letting go of each other's hands, so they end up standing back in the circle, facing either inwards or outwards.

Once they are untangled, ask them:

How did you work out the solution?

Answers could include co-operation, listening to each other, trying different ways and so on.

Evaluate the session using the Adult evaluation grid.

Copy onto card, laminate and cut each sheet into three cards, with one statement on each card.

A wants to watch a cartoon on television. B wants to watch a game show. The two programmes are both on at the same time.

A and B both want to read the same reading book.

A wants to play with B in the playground, but B is already playing with C.

PCM 12:
Homework sheet Session 3

Name: ....

Write in the petal an occasion since Session 3 when you might have fallen out with a friend, brother or sister, but you did something that solved the problem. Do not mention any names, just write 'someone'.

Your description should include:

- what the problem was
- what you did to solve the problem
- how the other person felt afterwards
- how you felt afterwards and why.

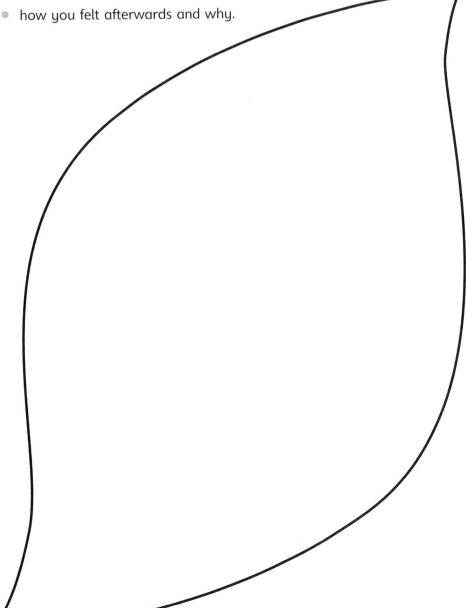

You may decorate your petal if you want.

Cut out your petal and bring it to our next session.

Session 4 Resolving conflict

Resources

- stickers • pencils • Choice cards (**PCM 13**) – one set per pair
- Base board (**PCM 14**) – one set per pair
- Homework sheet (**PCM 15**) – one per pupil
- Group contracts • Adult evaluation grids

Aims

- To recognise that there are different ways of dealing with a problem
- To reflect on their own ability to resolve problems in different ways
- To recognise, name and deal with their feelings in a positive way
- To think about themselves; to learn from their experiences and the experiences of others in developing relationships
- To encourage children to take responsibility for their own actions

Introduction 1 min.

Take the register, say hello to everyone, and remind them about the tick system.

Game: Dracula 5 mins.

This game is a group-building activity.

Sit in a circle. One child is chosen to be Dracula and stands in the centre. Dracula, with arms outstretched, points at them, names a seated child and walks in their direction. Before Dracula reaches them the victim must point to and name another child. Dracula then sets off to touch a new victim. The game continues until Dracula touches a victim before the victim names another child. The victim then becomes Dracula.

Give out ticks.

Recapping the contracts 5 mins.

This activity will reinforce the agreed way of working you have already established. Recap on the rules agreed in the contracts.

Give out the contracts. Award any stickers from the previous session to stick on their contracts.

End the activity by giving out ticks.

Review homework [10 mins.]

This activity practises communication skills and is an opportunity to share feelings and analyse situations.

Invite pupils to share how they resolved a difficulty during the week and

what the outcome was. For example, 'Someone in class didn't have any coloured pens, so I shared mine with them.'

Remind them not to use names, just 'someone'. Encourage them to give concrete descriptions of how they solved the problem; for example, 'We agreed to take it in turns.' Ask them how they felt when they had found a solution; for example, 'I felt pleased because I sorted things out.' You could also discuss how they thought the other person felt when the problem was solved. Praise thoughtfulness. Point out how the issue was resolved or managed in a controlled way.

Give out ticks for this activity.

Game: Oranges and Lemons [5 mins.]

This game, described in Session 1, concentrates on the skills needed to listen and keep each other safe, and provides a fun break.

Give out ticks at the end of the game.

Open forum [10 mins.]

This gives pupils an opportunity to explore different solutions to real problems, encouraging self-expression, problem-solving and listening skills. Use either A or B.

A: *Is any child unhappy because they are involved in a conflict and need help to resolve it?*

If so, ask them to explain the problem to the rest of the group. Remind them not to use names, just 'someone'.

Give the children, in pairs, two minutes to suggest together possible ways of resolving this conflict.

❝I've learned other ways of dealing with conflict, ways of talking and communication.❞

Hannah (10 yrs)

Bring the group back together and take suggestions, writing them on a master list for consideration. Possible suggestions include:

- Listen carefully to each other's point of view.

- Try to come to an agreement or compromise which you both feel comfortable with.

- Ask a mutually agreed third person to arbitrate. Who could that be?

- Capitulate – how important is the issue to you? ▶▶▶

▶▶▶

- If one party is being intractable and not really looking for a solution, they may need encouragement from you to consider their behaviour and think about why co-operation is desirable. That might be you!

Remind the children how they suggested ways of helping in Session 3, beginning 'Would it help if...'. Discuss the ideas on the list and ask pupils to make suggestions based on them.

B: Game: Choice cards with Base board

On the Base board are four different scenarios. The Choice cards describe different ways pupils could respond to each situation: three things they could do and three things they should do.

In pairs, pupils discuss the different scenarios and place the Choice cards in the most appropriate place on the Base board (5 mins.).

As a group, compare the pupils' responses and discuss any issues arising.

Remind the children:

You are responsible for your own responses/behaviour.
You can choose the way you respond.

Give out ticks for this part of the session.

Homework 5 mins.

This activity develops pupils' awareness of the process of making choices about their own behaviour.

Give out the Homework sheets.

Explain to pupils that before next time they need to write down an occasion when they responded in a different way from the way they might normally have behaved, as a result of the discussions in the group.

They should write down:

- what the situation was
- three different ways in which they could have dealt with the issue
- what they chose to do and why
- what the outcome was.

They should then decorate their petal, cut it out and bring it to the next session. Give out ticks.

End game: Tangles 5 mins.

This game, described in Session 3, concludes the session by encouraging co-operation and listening skills. You could extend the game by having one pupil outside the circle instructing the others how to untangle themselves.

Evaluate the session using the Adult evaluation grid.

PCM 13: Choice cards

Copy onto card, laminate and cut into individual cards,
one set for each pair of pupils.

✂

join in the fight	call your friends over to watch	make a circle around them and shout encouragement
call an adult	walk away from the fight	move away from the fight and carry on with your own game
start laughing and pointing	whisper to your friends to watch	join in messing around
ignore them	carry on with your own work	put up your hand and tell the adult
push them out of the way	shout at them	call them names
ask them to move	show them where the back of the line is	let them stay and tell the adult
tell them to go away	tell them that they're rubbish at games and you don't want them in your team	tell them you don't like them so they can't stay
let them join in	explain that the game has started but you will play with them at next break	point out other children who are free that they could play with

PCM 14: Base board

Copy onto card, laminate. One set for each pair of pupils.

Two pupils start fighting in the playground	
should do	could do

A pupil is messing around in class	
should do	could do

A pupil pushes in front of you in the line	
should do	could do

A pupil wants to join in your game	
should do	could do

PCM 15:
Homework sheet Session 4

Name: ....

Write in the petal an occasion since Session 4 when you responded in a different way from the way you might normally have behaved, as a result of the discussions we have had in our group.

Write down:

- what the situation was
- three different ways you could have dealt with the issue
- what you chose to do and why
- what the outcome was.

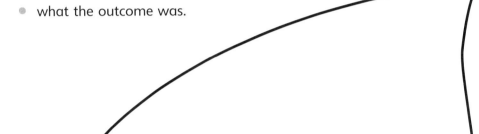

You can decorate your petal if you want.

Cut out your petal and bring it to our next session.

Permission to Photocopy

Session 5 No more disruption!

Resources

- stickers • whiteboard and pens • pencils • paper
- Pupil targets for class work (**PCM 16**) – one per pupil
- Homework sheet (**PCM 17**) – one per pupil
- Group contracts • Adult evaluation grids

Aims

- To reduce the level of disruption in the classroom
- To identify problems which stop the group from getting on with their work in class
- To consider the options when faced with problems that prevent them from getting on with their work
- To understand that they are responsible for their own behaviour

Introduction 1 min.

Take the register, say hello to everyone, and remind them about the tick system.

Game: Pass the Animal Noise 5 mins.

This game, described in Session 2, is a group-building activity.

Give out ticks for this part of the session.

Recapping the contracts 5 mins.

As before, this activity reinforces the agreed way of working in the group and develops communication skills.

Give out contracts. Recap on the rules agreed. Award any stickers from the previous session to stick on their contracts. Give out ticks for this part of the session.

Review homework 10 mins.

This activity practises communication skills and reinforces the idea that children can choose how to behave.

Pupils were asked to record three ways they could have chosen to deal with a situation. Each group member in turn recounts only what they chose to do and why.

▶▶▶

▶▶▶ At the end of the activity, remind the group:

- **You are responsible for your own behaviour.**
- **You can choose how you respond to a situation.**
- **Other people respond to your behaviour.**

Finish by giving out ticks.

Activity: Classroom disruption `15 mins.`

This activity encourages reflection and practises communication skills and taking turns.

What kind of problems might exist in the classroom which stop the class from working quietly?

Give children a couple of minutes to share their ideas, in pairs. Then ask each pair to report back to the group, and create a master list. Decide together:

Which ones are genuine difficulties and which ones are unnecessary interruptions?

Include:

- Don't know what to do
- Others talking
- Don't have the correct equipment
- Others being silly – ask them to define this.

For each item on the list, discuss:

Is this appropriate behaviour in class?

Give out paper or whiteboards. Give pupils five minutes to write down four examples of disruptive behaviour, either from the list or their own ideas. For each example, they should write:

- What I could do (wrong response)
- What I should do (appropriate response).

This activity may be undertaken orally and scribed by the adult. Bring the group together to share and discuss their ideas. Give out ticks for this activity.

Open forum `5 mins.`

This gives pupils a chance to explore different solutions to real problems, and encourages problem-solving and listening skills.

Ask if anyone has a different problem in the classroom which stops them from getting on with their work which they would like help with.

Remind them of the rule: no names; use 'someone'.

Invite other pupils to make suggestions, beginning 'Would it help if ...?' as practised in Sessions 3 and 4. Target pupil responses: 'Thank you, I will do that / I have done that.'

Give out ticks for this part of the session.

Game: Oranges and Lemons 5 mins.

This game, described in Session 1, concentrates on the skills needed to listen and keep each other safe.

Give out ticks at the end of the game.

Homework 5 mins.

This activity encourages children to focus on any of their own behaviour which may be disruptive for others, and how they can modify it.

Think of something you do which may stop the class from working quietly.

Give the pupils time to respond.

How can you change your behaviour so you don't disturb others?

Encourage pupils to frame this as a positive statement: 'To help the class work quietly this week I will ...'. This is their target.

Working around the group, each pupil generates their own target. The adult (or pupil) then writes the target on the Homework sheet.

Explain to pupils that during the week they need to write in their petal three times when they used their target behaviour. They should write down:

- what happened
- what they did to help the class work quietly
- how they felt afterwards.

They may then decorate and cut out the petal, and bring it to the next session.

Write each pupil's target on a pupil targets sheet. Explain to the children that the class teacher will have the sheets and will put a tick on them each day that the child achieves their target. You will see how many ticks they have gained in the next session. Give each child their sheet to hand to their class teacher.

Give out ticks for this activity.

End the session 5 mins.

Remind everyone that in the next session they will start making their flower posters. Ask them to think before they meet again about what they have learned from these sessions.

End the session by asking each child to state their next target, as a reminder. Then give out ticks.

Evaluate the session using the Adult evaluation grid.

PCM 16:
Pupil targets for class work

Name: ....

Date: ....

Dear ....,
To help the class work quietly this week I will ....

I will practise this once each day. Please put a tick for each day that you notice that my target has been achieved.

Monday	Tuesday	Wednesday	Thursday	Friday

Thank you.

PCM 17:
Homework sheet Session 5

Name:..

To help the class work quietly I will

....

Write in the petal three times when you did this.

Write down:

- what happened
- what you did to help the class work quietly
- how you felt afterwards.

Don't mention any names,
just call the person
'someone'.

You may decorate
your petal if you
want to.

Cut out your petal
and bring it to our
next session.

Session 6 Review

Resources

- stickers ● pupils' cut-out petals ● pencils and crayons
- glue ● scissors ● rulers
- Group contracts ● Self-portraits from Session 1
- assorted coloured card (A1 and A4)
- templates for poster (**PCM 18**, **PCM 19**, **PCM 20**)
- Pupil targets from Session 5, completed by the teacher
- Adult evaluation grids
- Example of completed poster (p. 49)

Aims

- To review the work completed during the five previous sessions and identify what each pupil has learned
- To begin the posters

Introduction 1 min.

Take the register, say hello to everyone. Remind pupils of the tick system.

Game: Whispers 5 mins.

This game is a group-building activity that encourages co-operation.

One pupil starts by whispering a short phrase in the ear of the next pupil, who whispers what they hear into the ear of the next pupil, and so on. The last person reveals what they think they heard. Play several rounds, with different pupils starting each time.

Give out ticks for this game.

Recapping the contracts 5 mins.

Give out the contracts. Recap on the rules agreed in the contracts with the children.

This activity establishes an agreed way of working co-operatively and develops communication skills.

Award any stickers from the previous session for children to stick on their contracts.

Give out ticks for this part of the session.

Review homework [10 mins.]

In this activity, pupils practise communication skills and listening to each other. Invite pupils in turn to tell the rest of the group their target for helping the class to work quietly, and describe one of the times when they achieved this that they have written about.

The adult should refer to the teacher's record and comment on the teacher's tick list, for example, **You obviously tried hard to remember to empty your book bag each day and I can tell that Miss Sinfield noticed because she gave you all these ticks. Well done.**

What differences did you notice when the class were working more quietly, and how did it help you?

Finish by giving out ticks.

> **❝ I enjoy playing fun games with everybody! ❞**
>
> *Katie (10 yrs)*

Discussion: What has been learned [5 mins.]

This activity encourages reflection and turn taking, and practises communication skills.

What do you think you have learned and will take away from the sessions?

In pairs, share ideas for a minute or so.

Come together as a group to report back. Note each pupil's response on the Adult evaluation grid.

Give out ticks for this activity.

> **❝ I've learned to be polite and give eye contact when we talk. ❞**
>
> *John (10 yrs)*

Activity: Begin posters [20 mins.]

This activity encourages pupils to reflect on their achievements and to recognise the positive changes they have made in their interactions with others.

Show the example of the completed poster. Explain the different elements of it: the petals, portrait, watering can and stem, and the templates for these.

Ask pupils to choose the colour A1 card they want to use for their poster. They may cut out their portrait and stick it on to the card, with their homework petals, to create the head of the flower.

Explain that they will finish the poster in the next session.

Game: Oranges and Lemons 5 mins.

This game, described in Session 1, concentrates on the skills needed to listen and keep each other safe, and provides an enjoyable concluding activity.

Give out ticks at the end of the game.

As the contracts have to be laminated for next week, award any stickers earned this week now.

Evaluate the session using the Adult evaluation grid for each pupil.

Copy onto card and cut out.

PCM 19: Stalk template

Copy onto card and cut out.

PCM 20:

Watering can template

Copy onto card and cut out.

Session 7 Growing flowers

Resources

- cut-out petals • pencils • coloured pens or crayons
- glue • scissors • rulers • glitter • self-portraits
- Group contracts • example of completed poster (p. 49)
- Pupil evaluation sheet (**PCM 21**) – one per pupil
- Adult evaluation grids
- fresh copy of Pupil questionnaire (**PCM 4**) – one per pupil
- Certificate of achievement (**PCM 22**) – one per pupil

Aims

- To work on the posters, reflect on how to keep the flower flourishing (the flower represents the individual pupil) and decide what should be written on the watering can to keep the flower alive
- To complete the Pupil evaluation sheets
- To thank the group for their participation and present them with their contracts

Introduction 1 min.

Take the register and say hello to everyone.

Game: Oranges and Lemons (5 mins.). This game, described in Session 1, encourages group bonding and relaxation. The group could nominate a pupil to explain the game and act as caller.

Recapping the contracts 2 mins.

Give out contracts. This activity establishes an agreed way of working co-operatively and develops communication skills. Recap on the rules agreed. Take the contracts back until later in the session.

Creating the flower poster 15 mins.

Review creating the poster in Session 6. Ask pupils to explain what they have done so far. Explain what they need to do next.

- Create a stem, plant pot and watering can for their flower, either using the templates provided or drawing freehand.
- Write their name on the pot and decorate it.

Discuss what needs to go into the watering can to help the flower grow well. Explain to the pupils that their flower represents them. The watering can represents all the new skills they have learned through the sessions, and they write these on the watering can. Invite pupils to suggest ideas, for example:

- 'I will think more about how other people feel.'
- 'I can use words instead of my hands to sort things out.'
- 'I will help people who are feeling sad.'

It is up to each child to decide what will help their flower (themselves) to grow and flourish. Pupils may write as many ideas as they wish on their watering can.

Pupils work at their own pace throughout the remainder of the session, with adult support as required, to complete their flowers.

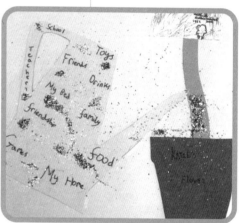

❝ I enjoyed working with the group. ❞

Rahul (9 yrs)

Presenting completed posters 5 mins.

This activity enhances self-esteem and is an opportunity to reflect on what each pupil has gained from the sessions. It also marks the beginning of the ceremonial ending of the programme.

Lay out the posters around the room and give the children time to look at, read and admire them.

The adult should encourage children's responses to the work they see with comments such as:

What do you like about this poster?

What do you think this person has learned about themselves?

How does your poster help you?

Ask pupils to think about what they will do with their posters. Some may be happy to have them displayed in school, or presented in a whole-school assembly, before taking them home. Some, however, may feel that the poster is very personal and prefer to take it home when the programme ends. Adults should emphasise that either decision is acceptable.

Activity: Pupil evaluation 10 mins.

This activity encourages self-evaluation and personal reflection. Give each pupil a Pupil evaluation sheet to complete. Ask them to complete the four statements on it:

- Something I learned ...
- Something I found difficult ...
- Something I would change ...
- Something I enjoyed ...

Bring the group together and invite each pupil in turn to read out their statements.

Acknowledge each pupil's evaluation by reflecting positively on their comments, for example:

You speak to your friends much more gently than you used to and I am sure that makes them listen to you more.

Ask pupils to repeat the Pupil questionnaire activity. They circle the picture that shows how they feel now about each statement.

Presenting the contracts 5 mins.

This activity recognises pupils' ability to follow rules, their capacity for change and their teamwork.

Thank the pupils for their efforts during the seven sessions.

Present each pupil with their contract. (If possible, get someone to laminate them during the session.) The adult may wish to comment on how well the pupils have worked together to keep to the rules, and to encourage them to continue to support each other in the classroom and playground.

66 I wouldn't change anything, I learned to listen and I am now confident in my work. 99

Sophie (9 yrs)

Activity: Celebrating achievement 5 mins.

This activity recognises the individual effort pupils have made and their contribution to the achievement of the group. Congratulate the group on how well they have worked together and individually, and present each child with their Certificate and if appropriate a small gift, to mark the end of the programme.

Game 5 mins.

Finish on a light-hearted note by playing the children's favourite game from previous sessions.

PCM 21:
Pupil evaluation sheet

Name: ....

Date: ....

Something I learned ...

Something I found difficult ...

Something I would change ...

Something I enjoyed ...

PCM 22:
Certificate of achievement

CERTIFICATE
OF
ACHIEVEMENT

Congratulations

....

You have successfully completed

....

Social Skills Programme.

Teacher .... Date ....

Adapting the group model for whole-class sessions

The content and order of the sessions is flexible and open to adaptation according to the needs of individual pupils. Additional sessions may also be incorporated.

These sessions may be used as they are or as a template for one-off sessions focusing on specific issues. In addition, the programme may be presented as a whole-class scheme of work for inclusion in PSHE.

The example below shows one way of adapting the group work from Session 5 into a whole-class session for a Year 5 class.

Note: If a member of the class has completed this session already in a small group, they could be part of the team delivering the session for the whole class and, in doing so, build self-esteem.

Year 5 Reflection time

Aims

- To reduce the level of disruption in the classroom
- To identify problems which stop the class from getting on with their work in class
- To consider the options when faced with problems that prevent them from getting on with their work
- To understand that they are responsible for their own behaviour

Resources

On each table:

- Pencils, paper, crayons or coloured pens
- The activity sheets for Reflection time
    - Classroom disturbances (**PCM 23**) – one for every three pupils
    - Ways of behaving in the classroom (**PCM 24**) – one per pupil
    - Targets (**PCM 25**) – one for every two pupils
- Whiteboard, paper and markers
- Blu-Tack®

Children should sit in groups at tables for this session.

Introduction 5 mins.

I am going to talk to you for a few minutes. I would like you to listen without interrupting me. There will be time for you to speak later.

Explain that there is a problem in the classroom which you need pupils' help to solve.

Many children have complained that they can't get on with their work in this classroom. There are lots of reasons for this.

- *Sometimes it is to do with the work.*
- *Sometimes it is to do with the children themselves.*
- *Sometimes it is to do with other children.*

Identifying the issues 10 mins.

Give the children a few minutes to think about things that happen in class which stop them getting on with their work. These might be:

- to do with the work
- to do with things they do themselves
- things that other children do.

Ask the children to write down all the things they can think of that stop them getting on with their work on a classroom disturbances slip. They should work on their own. Tell them not to worry about spelling, just write down what they think. Emphasise that they should not write names – use 'someone'.

Sharing ideas 20 mins.

Change the groups by moving some children, for example:

If your first name has an 'I' in it, stand up. Swap places by moving slowly and carefully without touching anyone else. Take your slip of paper with you.

Establish the rules for the rest of the session:

- Put up your hand to speak
- Take turns
- Listen when others are speaking
- No names – say 'someone'.

You may find it helpful to display these on a poster.

Divide the whiteboard into three sections:

Work	Things I do	Things other people do

▶▶▶

▶▶▶ In turn, each pupil says one thing that stops them from getting on with their work. Write each under the appropriate heading. Add ticks next to any item that is repeated.

Ask the children to look at the list and decide which problems are genuine difficulties (reasonable disruptions) and which are unnecessary.

Read each item in turn, asking children to vote with a show of hands on whether it is genuine or unnecessary.

On the whiteboard, underline genuine disruptions in blue and unnecessary disruptions in red.

Then ask the class to do the following:

1. On their own piece of paper mark the things they have written: ✓ for genuine and X for unnecessary.

2. Underline the things they know they have done which stop the class getting on with their work.

3. Think about which things are genuine and which things are unnecessary.

Ask the children to think about which thing on the class list or their own list causes the most disruption. Invite them to share their ideas.

Behaving in the classroom 10 mins.

Choose three examples of disruptive behaviour identified from the whiteboard.

Ask pupils to write one in each section of their copy of Ways of behaving in the classroom. For each example, they should write one idea in each of the sections:

- Things I could do

- Things I will do

Ask pupils: **What will you do to help solve the problem?** Go round the class, asking children to begin their suggestions with 'Would it help if I ...?'

Explain to the pupils:

- *You are responsible for your own behaviour.*

- *You can choose how you respond to a situation – you can choose how you behave.*

- *You make choices all the time. You can choose how to behave in class.*

- *With choices come responsibilities. If you choose to behave badly, you must accept the consequences.*

Setting personal targets 10 mins.

Give each child a Targets slip.

Ask them to identify one thing they could do in the next week which would help the class work quietly, and write this on their slip.

All the worksheets will go on display. After each lesson, I shall tick your sheet if you have helped to solve the problem. That is a possible 4 ticks each day until the end of the week. The most ticks you can get will be 20. Anyone with 15 ticks or more on Friday will get a special certificate. [This may be a head teacher's certificate or a class award, in line with the school policy.] *If the whole class gets a total of ... ticks* [a total of 75% of the class times 15]*, we may choose a class reward.*

End the session by reminding the children:

- *You can choose.*
- *You are responsible for your own behaviour.*

Just before the session ends, as a reminder, ask each child to say what they will do this week to help the class work quietly.

Classroom disturbances

✂ -

Name:...

Things that stop me from getting on with my work quietly:

- -

Name:...

Things that stop me from getting on with my work quietly:

- -

Name:...

Things that stop me from getting on with my work quietly:

- -

PCM 24:
Year 5 Reflection time

Ways of behaving in the classroom

Name: ....

1. ....

Things I could do

Things I will do

2. ....

Things I could do

Things I will do

3. ....

Things I could do

Things I will do

PCM 25:
Year 5 Reflection time
Targets

Year: .... Name: ....

To help the class work quietly this week I will

....

....

Signed: .... Date: ....

Monday	Tuesday	Wednesday	Thursday	Friday

Year: .... Name: ....

To help the class work quietly this week I will

....

....

Signed: .... Date: ....

Monday	Tuesday	Wednesday	Thursday	Friday